Read the story. Circle the correct answer for each sentence.

Jordan's Pets

Jordan likes reptiles even though many people do not. Jordan has a pet snake and a pet lizard at home. Her dad never comes into her room when her pets are out, but Jordan and her mom play with them all of the time. Jordan hopes to get a turtle for her birthday.

1. Jordan **(likes, dislikes)** reptiles.

2. A snake **(is, is not)** a reptile.

3. Jordan's mother **(likes, dislikes)** reptiles.

4. Jordan **(wants, does not want)** a turtle.

5. Jordan's father **(likes, dislikes)** snakes.

6. Everyone loves reptiles. **yes   no**

7. Jordan wants a pet rat. **yes   no**

8. A lizard is a reptile. **yes   no**

Elephants

What can weigh up to 14,000 pounds (6,350 kilograms) but only eats plants? A male African elephant! Elephants are herbivores. An adult elephant can eat about 300 pounds (136 kilograms) of food each day! African elephants have big ears that are shaped like the continent of Africa. African elephants have two "fingers" at the end of their trunks. They use these "fingers" to pick up things. Both male and female African elephants have large, visible tusks.

Two kinds of elephants are living today: African elephants and Asian elephants. Asian elephants are smaller and shorter than African elephants. They also weigh less. A male Asian elephant can weigh up to 11,000 pounds (4,990 kg). They also have smaller ears. They have high foreheads and one "finger" at the end of their trunks. Males have small tusks, and most females have no visible tusks.

African Elephant

Asian Elephant

Fill in the blanks.

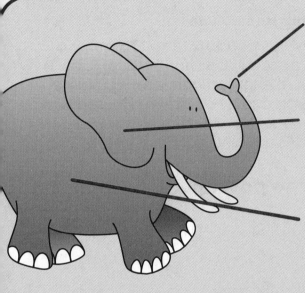

_____ "fingers" at the end of the trunk.

Ears are shaped like _____ _____ .

A male African elephant can weigh up to _____ pounds.

_____ "finger" at the end of the trunk.

Male Asian elephants have _____ tusks than male African elephants.

A male Asian elephant can weigh up to _____ pounds.

Read the passage. Follow the directions.

A Dinosaur Named Sue

What stands 13 feet (4 meters) tall and is 42 feet (13.8 m) long and is in Chicago, Illinois? It's a dinosaur fossil named Sue! Sue is a *Tyrannosaurus rex* skeleton. She is the largest and most complete *T. rex* ever found. Her skeleton is on display at the Field Museum. She was found after 67 million years. A fossil hunter named Sue Hendrickson uncovered her. That's how she got her name.

Circle the main idea of the passage.

There is a *T. rex* fossil named Sue in Chicago, Illinois.

Dinosaur fossils are hard to find.

Sue Hendrickson is a fossil hunter.

Underline each true statement.

1. Sue was named for the person who discovered her.

2. It is easy to find complete dinosaur fossils.

3. Sue is on display at the Field Museum.

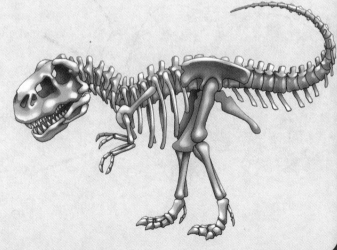

Circle the words hidden in the puzzle. Words can be found across, down, and diagonally.

Word Bank

claws	dinosaur	extinct	fossil
hunter	jaws	skeleton	Sue

```
s  j  x  c  l  a  w  s  d  l  w
d  k  h  u  n  t  e  r  i  z  r
m  e  e  n  o  y  r  v  n  a  v
h  x  f  l  p  b  s  r  o  q  t
x  t  s  o  e  h  e  q  s  m  o
q  i  z  e  s  t  n  o  a  k  j
k  n  b  g  n  s  o  p  u  k  a
v  c  u  a  o  i  i  n  r  o  w
w  t  r  a  s  u  e  l  y  c  s
```

My Backyard Bunny

Mr. Wiggins is my rabbit. He lives in my backyard. He likes to hide in the bushes. He also hides behind the flowerpots. He pretends that he is wild and eats the grass, but he likes the vegetables and fruits we leave out for him too. He even likes to eat crackers and cereal. Sometimes, he lets me rub his head. He is not really wild.

1. What is the name of the rabbit? _____

   _____

2. Where does the rabbit like to hide? _____

   _____

Answer each question from the story on page 6.

3. What does the rabbit eat? _____

_____

4. Why do you think the author says that this rabbit is not

really wild? _____

_____

5. Does the author like the rabbit? How do you know? _____

_____

_____

6. Do you think this rabbit would be a good pet? Why or why not?

_____

_____

_____

Tennis Basics

Tennis is played on a flat, rectangular area called a court. Most courts are outside. A tennis court's size is different for singles (two players) and doubles (four players). The court's boundaries are marked with white lines. A net stretches across the middle of the court to divide it in half. There is a forecourt and a backcourt on each side of the net.

Tennis is played with a strung racket and a hollow rubber ball covered with fuzzy cloth. Players on either side of the net hit the ball back and forth. Tennis matches are divided into either three or five sets. Only four points are needed to win each game. But, a player must win at least six games to win a set.

Word Bank

backcourt   Doubles   match   net
rectangular   six   Tennis

Across

4. The shape of a tennis court
5. A tennis _____ is divided into three or five sets.
6. A _____ divides the tennis court in half.
7. _____ is usually played outside.

Down

1. Each side of a tennis court has a forecourt and a _____.
2. _____ means that there are four players.
3. A tennis player must win _____ games to win a set.

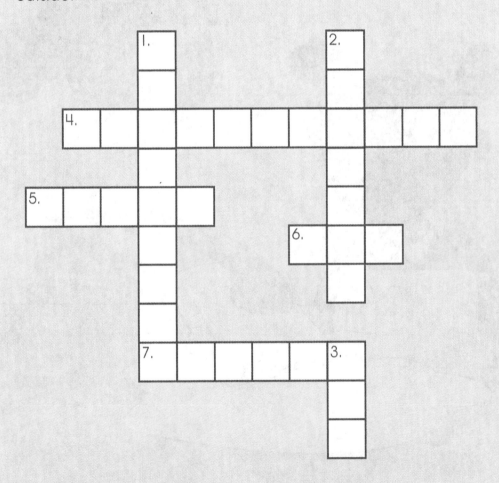

Spilled Milk

Hannah was reading on the porch. She thought she heard someone crying in the kitchen. She got up to check. Her little sister had spilled her glass of milk. Hannah smiled and gave her sister a big hug. Her sister stopped crying and asked for another glass of milk. Hannah helped her sister clean up the mess. Hannah poured her sister another glass of milk.

Answer each question from the story on page 10.

1. What caused Hannah to stop reading and go to the kitchen?

   _____

2. What effect did hugging her sister have? _____

   _____

3. What caused Hannah to pour her sister another glass of milk? _____

   _____

4. What effect do you think this accident had on the way Hannah's

   sister will drink her next glass of milk? _____

   _____

Write a paragraph about a time when you spilled something. What caused the spill, and what effect did it have on you?

_____

_____

_____

_____

_____

Read the story. Number the events in the correct order.

A Walk Around the Block

Tasha went for a walk around the neighborhood with her uncle. She stopped and pointed at many things that she saw along the way.

She saw an ant carry a tiny leaf across the sidewalk. She saw a bird in a tree. She saw an odd-shaped rock in the grass.

When they got back home, her uncle laughed and said, "That was not much of a walk. It was more like a look!"

____ Tasha saw a rock in the grass.

____ Tasha saw a bird in a tree.

____ Tasha and her uncle went for a walk.

____ Tasha's uncle made a joke.

____ Tasha watched an ant carry a leaf.

CD-104369

Read each sentence beginning. Circle the letter of the correct ending for each sentence.

1. When Tasha's uncle takes her for a walk around the neighborhood again, her uncle will probably . . .

    A. plan more time for the walk.

    B. bring an umbrella on the walk.

    C. wear gloves.

2. The objects that Tasha sees on the walk prove that Tasha was looking . . .

    A. up only.

    B. down only.

    C. both up and down.

Draw a picture of something you might see on your next neighborhood walk.

Read the passage. Circle the letter of the correct word or phrase to complete each sentence.

King Arthur

A legend says that England once had a noble king named Arthur who fought for good and decent things. He defeated his foes and won the respect of his people. His court was in a place called Camelot. He had meetings there with his knights at a round table. The shape of the table meant that no one was at the head of the table.

King Arthur and his knights were known for their kindness and gentleness. The legend says that King Arthur brought order and peace to his kingdom during the Middle Ages.

1. A legend says that Arthur was a _____.

   A. sword

   B. king

   C. knight

2. King Arthur's court was called _____.

   A. Camelot

   B. Charlotte

   C. Canada

3. King Arthur and his knights sat at a _____ table.

   A. square

   B. oval

   C. round

4. The shape of the table meant that _____.

   A. everyone was comfortable

   B. no one was at the head of the table

   C. the king was their leader

5. King Arthur brought _____ to his kingdom.

   A. peace

   B. money

   C. sadness

6. King Arthur ruled during the _____.

   A. Stone Age

   B. Dark Ages

   C. Middle Ages

CD-104369

Refer to the passage on page 14. Write the correct word or words next to each meaning.

Word Bank

decent	foes	kingdom
legend	Middle Ages	noble

1. enemies _____

2. honorable or respectable _____

3. a country with a king or queen _____

4. a time in history _____

5. myth _____

6. good _____

Fairy Tales

Come, read with me a fairy tale.
Board my ship, and we'll set sail.

Let's go to once upon a time,
Where good is good and all words rhyme.

Follow me to places far
Beyond the moon, beyond the stars.

We'll travel to lands far away,
Where wild creatures hide and play.

We'll pretend that we're sailors at sea,
Having adventures, wild and free.

Things here are not as they seem.
This place is only in our dreams.

Answer each question from the story on page 16.

1. What is a fairy tale?

   A. a make-believe story   B. a lie

   C. a story about fairies   D. a story written by fairies

2. Some words have more than one meaning. Read each sentence. Write the letter of the correct definition for each underlined word.

   ___ We used boards to build the ship.

   ___ The man boards the ship with his bags.

   A. to get on a ship

   B. pieces of wood

   ___ The star twinkled in the sky.

   ___ He is the star of the show.

   C. a light in the sky

   D. the main performer

   ___ They set sail for a long trip over the ocean.

   ___ They made a sail for their boat.

   E. a piece of material used to propel a boat

   F. to float on the water

3. Write the singular form of each word.

   creatures _____   sailors _____

   fairies _____   places _____

Cockroaches

Cockroaches have been on Earth for millions of years. They were here before the dinosaurs. They have hard shells that act like armor. They have good hearing and eyesight. Some mother cockroaches give birth to live young. Others lay eggs. Cockroaches eat almost anything but can live three months without food. They can even live 30 days without water. Cockroaches do not bite humans. So, why do people scream and run when they see them?

Circle F if the sentence is a fact. Circle O if the sentence is an opinion.

1. Cockroaches have hard shells.   **F**   **O**

2. Cockroaches have good eyesight.   **F**   **O**

3. Cockroaches are ugly.   **F**   **O**

4. Cockroaches eat almost anything.   **F**   **O**

5. Cockroaches do not bite humans.   **F**   **O**

List one detail in each oval to complete the story web. The main idea and one detail have been done for you.

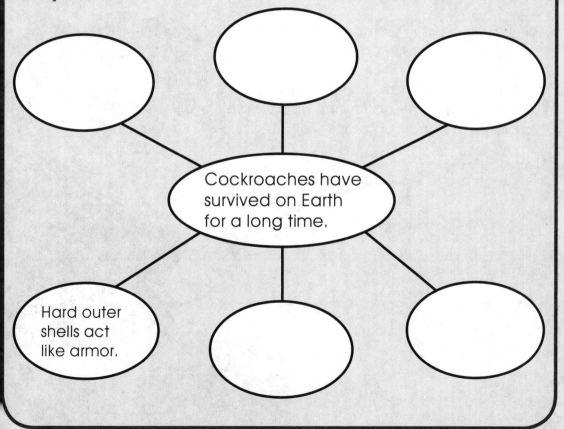

     CD-104369   **19**

Going Fishing!

Antonio was so excited that he could hardly fall asleep. He and his dad had been busy all day. First, they went out to breakfast and ordered pancakes. Next, they went to a big outdoor supplies store. Antonio and his dad bought some fishing line, sinkers, and hooks. They also bought Antonio a new rod. Then, the two went shopping for some fishing clothes. They bought a pair of shorts and a T-shirt for each of them. Finally, Antonio and his dad hunted in the dirt for worms. Antonio and his dad were going fishing tomorrow.

1. Underline in red the sentence that tells what Antonio and his dad did first.

2. Underline in blue the sentence that tells what happened next.

3. Underline in green the sentence that tells what Antonio and his dad finally did.

4. Underline in yellow the sentence that tells what Antonio and his dad are planning to do.

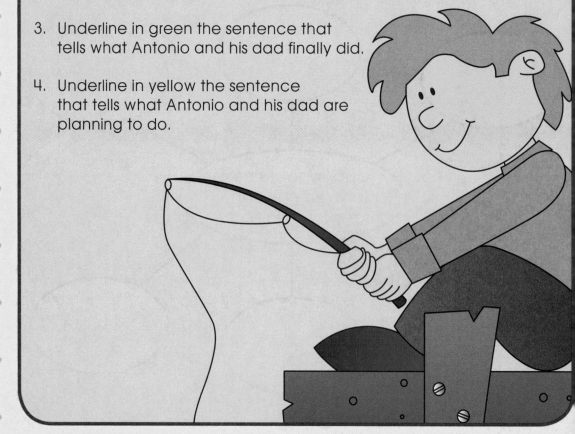

Answer each question from the story on page 20.

5. List three things that Antonio and his dad did before they went fishing. _____

_____

6. List four things that Antonio and his dad bought. _____

_____

7. Do you think that Antonio was excited about this trip? Why? _____

_____

_____

In the space below, draw a picture of what you would want to take on a fishing trip.

Together Again

Oscar and Clarice were brother and sister. They lived in the same room at the animal shelter. Oscar was a big, loud kitten. Clarice was tiny and shy. One day, Raymond and his father went to the animal shelter to adopt a kitten. Raymond liked Oscar, but his father thought Clarice would make a better pet. They brought Clarice home, but she was not happy. She hid behind everything, meowed all night, and would not eat. The next day, Raymond and his dad went back to the shelter. They decided to adopt Oscar too.

Answer each question from the story on page 22.

1. How was Oscar different from Clarice? _____

_____

_____

2. If Raymond liked Oscar, why did he bring home Clarice? _____

_____

_____

3. What happened when Clarice wasn't with Oscar? _____

_____

_____

4. Why did Raymond and his dad go back to the shelter to get Oscar?

_____

_____

5. What do you think will happen now that Oscar and Clarice are

together again? _____

_____

_____

_____

Mars

Have you heard of the red planet? Sometimes, you can see it from Earth without a telescope. It's Mars, the fourth planet from the sun and Earth's neighbor. Earth is the third planet from the sun. From Earth, Mars appears to have a red color.

Mars moves around the sun in an oval orbit. A year on Mars takes about 687 Earth days. That's how long it takes for Mars to move around the sun. Earth takes 365 days to orbit the sun. So if you are 8 years old on Earth, you might be only 4 years old on Mars!

Scientists have found that Earth and Mars have conditions more similar to each other than to any other planet. But there are some big differences in the conditions on Mars. The atmosphere is mostly carbon dioxide. It has very little oxygen. There is very little water that we know of on Mars. Some scientists still believe there is life on Mars.

Circle the letter of each correct answer.

1. Mars is a _____ in our solar system.
   A. planet
   B. star
   C. galaxy
   D. meteor

2. If you are 8 years old on Earth, you would be _____ years old on Mars.
   A. 16
   B. 687
   C. 365
   D. 4

3. The conditions on Mars are most similar to _____.
   A. Neptune
   B. Earth
   C. Mercury
   D. Venus

4. From Earth, Mars appears to be _____.
   A. red
   B. blue
   C. white
   D. black

5. There is very little _____ on Mars.
   A. weather
   B. water
   C. time
   D. heat

First-Time Skater

Hector went skating for the first time on Saturday. He was really scared and held on tightly to his friend's hand. Hector was afraid he would fall, and he did fall a few times. Finally, he skated around the entire skating rink, then stopped to rest. He did this again and again for more than an hour. Then, it was time to go home.

Hector quickly took off his skates and put them on the counter. His friend felt bad that he was leaving. She thought that Hector did not have a good time. She asked him if he wanted to go skating again sometime. His friend was surprised when Hector said with a great big smile, "How about tomorrow?"

Fill in the blanks to complete the summary of the story.

The main character is _____ . He went _____ with

his friend. He was afraid because _____

_____ . His friend helped

him by _____ .

Hector and his friend planned to _____

_____ .

Why was Hector's friend surprised to hear that Hector wanted to go skating again?

_____

_____

_____

_____

_____

_____

_____

Read each statement. Before reading, check whether you think each statement is true or false. Next, read the passage on page 29. After reading, check true or false in the boxes on the right.

Before Reading:
True/False

After Reading:
True/False

☐ ☐ Hamsters are related to rats. ☐ ☐

☐ ☐ Hamsters sleep at night. ☐ ☐

☐ ☐ Hamsters have good eyesight. ☐ ☐

☐ ☐ Hamsters have good hearing. ☐ ☐

☐ ☐ Hamsters do not like loud noises. ☐ ☐

☐ ☐ Hamsters gnaw on things to sharpen their teeth. ☐ ☐

What did you learn?

_____

_____

_____

_____

_____

   CD-104369

Follow the directions on page 28 before reading the passage.

Hamsters

Hamsters are wild in some parts of the world, but they can make good pets. Hamsters are fun to watch and easy to handle. Hamsters are related to mice and rats. They belong to an animal family called rodents. Rodents have front teeth that continue to grow throughout their lives. They gnaw on things to stop their front teeth from getting too long. Hamsters are nocturnal. This means that they sleep in the day and stay awake at night. Hamsters have poor eyesight. If you stood more than a few steps from one, it would probably not see you. Hamsters have very good hearing and do not like sudden or loud noises. Hamsters recognize things by how they smell rather than how they look.

Talking Birds

I love to listen to parrots talk. They can copy the sounds that people make, but no one knows how they do it. Some scientists believe that parrots talk because they need to feel a close bond or friendship with other creatures or their owners. In the wild, parrots copy the sounds of other parrots. Bird owners believe that parrots know what is being said to them. Some scientists think that it is just luck when a parrot says the right word at the right time. They believe that it is learned behavior. For example, when some parrots hear a knock on the door, they may automatically say, "Hello!" Parrots also copy humans in other ways. Humans hold food in one hand and bring it to their mouths. Parrots hold food in one foot and bring it to their beaks.

Page 1

1. likes
2. is
3. likes
4. wants
5. dislikes
6. no
7. no
8. yes

Page 3

African Elephant: 2; the continent of Africa; 14,000

Asian Elephant: 1; smaller; 11,000

Page 4

Main idea: There is a T. rex fossil named Sue in Chicago, Illinois. Numbers 1 and 3 should be underlined.

Page 5

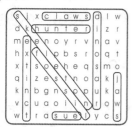

Page 6

1. Mr. Wiggins
2. in the bushes and behind the flowerpots

Page 7

3. grass, vegetables, fruits, crackers, cereal
4. The rabbit lets the author rub his head.
5.–6. Answers will vary.

Page 9

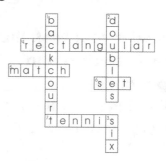

Page 11

1. She heard someone crying.
2. Her sister stopped crying.
3. She asked for another glass of milk.
4. Answers will vary but may include: She will be more careful next time.

Paragraphs will vary.

Page 12

4, 3, 1, 5, 2

Page 13

1. A.; 2. C.

Pictures will vary.

Page 14

1. B.; 2. A.; 3. C.; 4. B.; 5. A; 6. C.

Page 15

1. foes; 2. noble; 3. kingdom; 4. Middle Ages; 5. legend; 6. decent

A

Page 17
1. A.; 2. B.; A.; C.; D.; F.; E.;
3. creature, sailor, fairy, place

Page 19
1. F, 2. F, 3. 0, 4. F, 5. F,
Story webs will vary.

Page 20
1. Underlined in red: First, they went out to breakfast and ordered pancakes.
2. Underlined in blue: Next, they went to a big outdoor supplies store.
3. Underlined in green: Finally, Antonio and his dad hunted in the dirt for worms.
4. Underlined in yellow: Antonio and his dad were going fishing tomorrow.

Page 21
5. Answer should include three of the following: ate breakfast, went shopping for fishing supplies, went shopping for clothes, hunted for worms.
6. Answer should include four of the following: fishing line, sinkers, hooks, rod, shorts, and T-shirts.
7. Answers will vary.
Pictures will vary.

Page 23
1. Oscar was big and loud. Clarice was tiny and shy.
2. His dad thought that Clarice would make a better pet.
3. Clarice hid, meowed all night, and wouldn't eat.
4. Clarice was unhappy without Oscar.
5. Answers will vary.

Page 25
1. A.; 2. D.; 3. B.; 4. A.; 5. B.

Page 27
The main character is <u>Hector</u>. He went <u>skating</u> with his friend. He was afraid because <u>he thought he would fall</u>. His friend helped him by <u>holding on tightly to his hand</u>. Hector and his friend planned to <u>go skating again tomorrow</u>.
Answers will vary.

Page 28
Hamsters are related to rats. T
Hamsters sleep at night. F
Hamsters have good eyesight. F
Hamsters have good hearing. T
Hamsters do not like loud noises. T
Hamsters gnaw on things to sharpen their teeth. F
Answers will vary.

Page 31
1. Parrots
2. talk
3. scientists
4. owners
5. know
6. saying
7. learned
8. copy

Page 33
The first five sentences are supporting details (SD). The last sentence is the main idea (M). Answers will vary.

Page 35
1. T; 2. F; 3. F; 4. T; 5. T; 6. T; 7. T; Answers will vary but may include: As a fish lets water in its mouth, the water flows over the gills and the fish's body gets oxygen.

Page 37
8, 3, 1, 2, 6, 4, 5, 7
Answers will vary.

Page 39
1. to celebrate her birthday
2. surprised
3. She looked tired.
4. They knew that she loves playing softball and would like the food that they brought.

Page 39, continued
5. Answers can include: made waffles; went on a picnic; let her take a nap; cleaned the house; made dinner; did laundry; washed and put away the dishes; put on a skit.
6. Answers will vary.

Page 41
1. Answers will vary.
2. Answer should include three of the following: woke up late, rushed through breakfast, dropped homework in mud, wore two different-colored socks, best friend not at school, had to babysit sister, clean up puppy's mess, no potatoes at dinner, TV show cancelled, lots of homework.
3.–5. Answers will vary.

Page 43
1. B.; 2. F, T, F, T
3. elephant: in a group
sea otter: floating on its back
bat: upside down
flamingo: standing on one foot
squirrel: in a nest in a tree
4. Answers will vary.

Page 45
1. B.; 2. C.; 3. C.; 4. B.
5. He invented chewing gum.
6. Answers will vary.

C

Page 47
1. C.; 2. D.; 3. A.; 4. C.
5. Answers will vary.

Page 49
Answers will vary.
1. baseball
2. clues
3. sandwiches
4. playing
5. drink
6. afternoon

Page 51

Animal	Description of Egg	Where Egg Is Laid or Placed
male sea horse	soft-shelled	in pouch
most birds	hard-shelled	in nest of twigs
penguin	hard-shelled	on father's feet
octopus	long strands	roof of underwater cave
insects	in sacs	attached to leaves
fish	soft-shelled	in water

Pictures will vary.

Page 53
1. Ruth had a hard time seeing the board in class.
2. She used a machine and Ruth read letters on the wall.
3. They examine people's eyes.
4. The letters became clear and easy to read.
5. They help people pick out frames for their glasses.
6. Yes
7. Because Rosa did not need to read the board for Ruth anymore.

Page 55
1. Emma wanted to make dolls to sell.
2. She loves all of her dolls.
3.–4. Answers will vary.

Page 57
1. They set up the tent and unpacked the supplies for dinner.
2. They went to the creek.
3. He jumped into the tent and closed the flap.
4. Answers will vary.

Page 59
1. local; 2. eternity; 3. sobbed;
4. train; 5. competition;
6. announced; 7. embarrassed;
8. stubborn
Answers will vary.

Page 60
1. park; 2. pet; 3. rock; 4. crack;
5. stick; 6. watch

Use words from the Word Bank to fill in each blank.

Word Bank

copy	know	learned	owners
Parrots	saying	scientists	talk

_(1.)_ are interesting birds. They can _(2.)_ but, _(3.)_ do not know why or how. Bird _(4.)_ believe their birds _(5.)_ what they are _(6.)_ . Some scientists believe it is just _(7.)_ behavior. Parrots seem to like to _(8.)_ people.

1. _____

2. _____

3. _____

4. _____

5. _____

6. _____

7. _____

8. _____

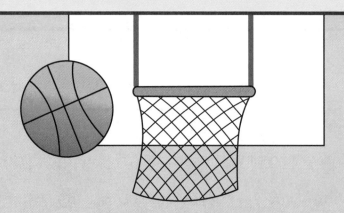

An American Custom?

Alexander is new to the United States. He and his family moved here from Kosovo. So far, he really likes his new country. He has learned English quickly and has made many friends. He studies hard and makes good grades in school.

There is just one thing that puzzles him. Everyone he meets says, "You must be a basketball player." Alexander is very tall for someone who is only 14 years old. But, he doesn't care that much about basketball. He actually likes soccer better. So, why does everyone want him to be a basketball player? The only thing he can figure out is that if an American person is tall, people think that he should play basketball. What a strange custom!

Write **M** next to the sentence that is the main idea of the story. Write **SD** next to the sentences that are supporting details in the story.

____ Alexander is from Kosovo.

____ Alexander likes to play soccer.

____ Alexander learned how to speak English and does very well in school.

____ Alexander is very tall for his age.

____ Alexander is 14 years old.

____ Alexander cannot understand why everyone expects him to be a basketball player.

Alexander wonders why everyone wants him to be a basketball player. How would you answer Alexander's question?

_____

_____

_____

_____

Read the passage. Follow the directions on page 35.

Fish

Fish are made just right for living underwater. They have sleek bodies to help them move. Their tail fins push them through the water. Their other fins help them steer or stop.

Most fish have skin that is covered with scales. These hard, clear scales help the fish swim too. Scales help the fish slide easily through the water.

Fish have gills for breathing. A fish opens its mouth and lets water in. When the fish closes its mouth, the water flows over the gills inside its body. A fish's body takes the oxygen it needs from the water.

Fish are cold-blooded. This means that a fish's body temperature matches the temperature of the water around it. Sharks are the only fish with eyelids. Other fish do not have eyelids. The water keeps their eyes washed. The underwater world is perfect for fish.

CD-104369

Circle **T** if the sentence is true. Circle **F** if the sentence is false.

1. Most fish have scales.   T F

2. Fish have lungs.   T F

3. Fish are warm-blooded.   T F

4. Most fish do not have eyelids.   T F

5. Tail fins push fish through the water.   T F

6. Fins help a fish steer.   T F

7. Fish have sleek bodies.   T F

Explain how a fish breathes.

_____

_____

_____

_____

_____

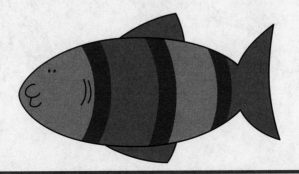

Jenny's Game

Jenny is teaching her friends how to play a game that she learned at camp. To play the game, she chooses one player to be "It," and her friends make a big circle around that player. Then, she ties a scarf in a knot and places it on the ground in the middle of the circle. Next, she asks the player who is "It" to say the name of a player to be "Challenger." Then, both players try to grab the scarf first. The player who grabs the scarf has to run to the empty spot in the circle left by "Challenger" without being tagged by the other player. If a person gets tagged, he becomes "It" for the next round. The game ends after everyone has had a turn.

Number the steps of the game in the correct order.

____ The game ends when everyone has had a turn.

____ Put the scarf in the center of the circle.

____ Choose one player to be "It."

____ Form a circle around "It."

____ The player who grabs the scarf runs to an empty spot in the circle.

____ Pick a "Challenger" to go in the circle with "It."

____ Both players try to grab the scarf.

____ If a person gets tagged, he becomes "It" for the next round.

What could you do to make this game more fun?

_____

_____

_____

_____

_____

_____

_____

Mrs. Foster's Big Day

Mrs. Foster's family wanted her 40th birthday to be great, but they did not have much money. So, they made her homemade waffles for breakfast. For lunch, they took a picnic to the ballpark because she loves playing softball. They brought tomato sandwiches and fresh fruit because they knew she would like that.

When they went home, they thought Mrs. Foster looked tired, so they put a pillow under her head and let her take a nap. Then, her family made dinner, did the laundry, and cleaned the house. Mrs. Foster was surprised.

After dinner, they washed the dishes and put them away. Mrs. Foster thanked her family. Then, her son and daughter asked her to sit on the couch while they put on a skit. Mrs. Foster laughed and said that this was her best birthday ever!

Answer each question from the story on page 38.

1. What did Mrs. Foster's family plan? _____

_____

2. How did Mrs. Foster feel when her family made dinner, did the

laundry, and cleaned the house? _____

_____

3. Why did her family let Mrs. Foster take a nap? _____

_____

4. Why did Mrs. Foster's family go on a picnic instead of to a

restaurant? _____

_____

5. List some of the things that her family did because they wanted to

make Mrs. Foster happy. _____

_____

6. How would you like to spend your perfect birthday? _____

_____

_____

_____

_____

Luis's Terrible Day

Luis was having a terrible day. He woke up late for school and had to rush through breakfast. He ate only one bite of toast before the bus arrived. On his way to the bus, he dropped his homework in the mud and noticed that he was wearing two different-colored socks. His best friend was not at school that day. That meant they could not share dessert at lunch. He always counted on that.

When Luis got home, he found out that he had to babysit his little sister and clean up the mess that his puppy made in the kitchen. Dinner was a big disappointment too. His dad had not made any potatoes. Luis loved potatoes. His favorite TV show was canceled because of a special report, and his homework took twice as long as usual. Luis was looking forward to bedtime.

Answer each question from the story on page 40.

1. Why do you think that Luis was looking forward to going to bed?

   _____

   _____

2. Name three things that happened to Luis to make his day terrible.

   _____

   _____

   _____

3. What might have caused Luis to wake up late for school? _____

   _____

   _____

4. Why do you think that Luis's best friend was not at school? _____

   _____

   _____

5. Have you had a day like Luis? What happened? _____

   _____

   _____

   _____

Animals' Sleeping Habits

Most humans sleep on a bed or a mat. Animals, however, have many different ways of sleeping.

Some animals sleep in groups for warmth. Lions, monkeys, and penguins are a few animals that sleep in groups. Elephants sleep in groups for protection. Larger, older elephants make a circle around the younger elephants. The younger elephants get inside the circle and lie down to sleep. The larger elephants sleep standing up.

Some animals sleep in trees. Birds lock their feet onto branches to keep them from falling out of the trees. Other animals, like squirrels and baboons, sleep in nests that they build in trees. They curl up to keep warm. Bats hang upside down from tree branches to sleep.

Most animals look for warm, dry places to sleep. But, ducks often sleep in the water. Sea otters sleep in the water too. They float on their backs in the seaweed.

Most animals lie down to sleep. However, some large animals, like horses, sleep standing up. Flamingos sleep standing on just one of their two legs.

Most animals sleep at night, but some animals are nocturnal. Nocturnal animals sleep during the day. Bats are nocturnal. They wake up when the sun goes down.

Animals sleep in different places and in different ways. But, just like humans, every animal must sleep.

Answer each question from the story on page 42.

1. Circle the letter of the sentence that tells the main idea of this passage.

   A. Most humans sleep on a bed or a mat.

   B. Animals have many different ways of sleeping.

   C. Most animals sleep all night.

2. Write **T** if the sentence is true. Write **F** if the sentence is false.

   ____ All animals sleep at night.

   ____ Elephants sleep in groups for protection.

   ____ Birds are the only animals that build nests.

   ____ All animals sleep.

3. Draw a line to match each animal with the way it sleeps.

   elephant   standing on one foot

   sea otter   in a nest in a tree

   bat   upside down

   flamingo   floating on its back

   squirrel   in a group

4. Where do you sleep? _____

_____

Chewing Gum

My name is Thomas Adams. You probably have no idea who I am, but I invented chewing gum. Well, invented might be a strong word.

I lived in the 1800s. I once met General Santa Anna. He was a Mexican general who told me about a dried sap called chicle. He liked to chew this sap that came from the sapodilla tree. He said that the Mayan civilization had been chewing it for hundreds of years. I tried some. Honestly, I thought it tasted terrible.

Still, I was interested in chicle because it was so rubbery. I thought that maybe I could make things like toys or boots out of it. But nothing I tried seemed to work. It would not replace rubber.

One day, I popped a terrible-tasting piece of chicle into my mouth and chewed and chewed. Yuck, I thought. It would be nice if it had some flavor. Eureka! I had a great idea! I opened a flavored-gum factory and sold a huge amount of chewing gum.

Americans loved my gum. But, doctors seemed to think that it was bad for your teeth. That may be true, but one doctor even said, "Chewing gum will exhaust the salivary glands and cause intestines to stick together." Isn't that the silliest thing that you have ever heard?

I am proud to say that flavored chewing gum was a hit! But why doesn't anyone know my name?

Answer each question from the story on page 44.

1. At the beginning of the story, how does the author feel about chicle?

   A. angry

   B. curious

   C. bored

2. How does the author feel about flavored chewing gum?

   A. embarrassed

   B. worried

   C. proud

3. What did the author think that the chicle could do?

   A. ruin teeth

   B. become rubber

   C. replace rubber

4. What does the author think about what one doctor said?

   A. It was right.

   B. It was silly.

   C. It was good.

5. Why does the author think that people should know his name?

   _____

6. Write a brief summary of this story. _____

   _____

   _____

   _____

Simpson's Ice-Cream Shop

Tyler's family opened an ice-cream shop. Tyler's dad made it a cheerful, fun place for families to go. He chose white tables and chairs with red designs. The menus had pictures of ice-cream cones, sundaes, and banana splits on them.

Sometimes, Tyler's family went to the shop to greet customers and check on business. Tyler was excited to sample ice-cream flavors while his parents talked to customers. Everyone always seemed to be enjoying the ice cream treats.

One evening, Tyler saw his soccer coach having a banana split. He ran over to say hello.

"Hi, Coach Kern!" Tyler said.

"Hello, Tyler. My son Owen said that you are here sometimes. How is it to have the most popular ice-cream shop in town?" asked Coach Kern.

"It's great! We are glad everyone likes our ice cream so much," said Tyler.

"This was the best banana split I ever had! It was great seeing you," said Coach Kern.

"I will tell my dad that you came by. Come back soon," Tyler said.

"I sure will," replied the coach as he left.

Tyler looked around the busy shop and beamed with pride. Even his coach had come to the shop! Tyler went to find his dad and share the news.

Answer each question from the story on page 46.

1. How did Tyler's dad believe that ice-cream shops should be?
   A. small and quiet
   B. colorful and quiet
   C. cheerful and fun
   D. crowded and noisy

2. Why was Tyler excited about visiting the shop?
   A. to talk to all of the customers
   B. to see his father
   C. to work at the shop
   D. to sample ice cream flavors

3. Why did the family go to "check on business?"
   A. to see if many people are there and if they are happy
   B. to see if the shop is open
   C. to see if the banana splits are good
   D. to let Tyler work there

4. Why do you think that Tyler was happy to see his soccer coach?
   A. because he likes ice cream
   B. because he told him he wanted to practice
   C. because he was proud his coach was visiting his dad's shop
   D. because he was hoping to play more soccer this year

5. In the space below, write the directions for making the best ice-cream treat that you can think of. Be sure to put the steps in the correct order.

_____

_____

Who Did It?

Caleb and Matt were playing baseball in Matt's backyard with some friends. They had been playing all afternoon in the hot sun.

Matt said, "I'm going inside to get a drink." The other boys went inside too.

The boys stayed inside to cool off. Soon, it was time for everyone to go home for lunch. Matt said that he was headed to the kitchen to get a snack. Matt's mother was already in the kitchen.

"Who ate all of the sandwiches?" she exclaimed. "They were right here on the counter."

Caleb and Matt looked at each other. "Not us, Mom," Matt said.

"Somebody must have. Do you have any clues?" Matt's mom said.

They looked around the kitchen for clues. The mud from the boys' shoes had left tracks on the floor. But, the tracks were nowhere near the counter where Matt's mom had put the sandwiches. They heard what sounded like a satisfied groan from the den. The three of them walked into the den to find . . .

Answer each question from the story on page 48.

Who ate the sandwiches? Write an ending for the story.

_____

_____

_____

_____

_____

Use the word bank to help you unscramble the words.

Word Bank

afternoon	baseball	clues
drink	playing	sandwiches

1. bleaslab _____

2. sceul _____

3. wicsseadnh _____

4. nailypg _____

5. kindr _____

6. nooterfan _____

All About Eggs

Most people know that chickens come from eggs. Did you know that many other animals also come from eggs? Eggs come in all sizes, from microscopic to large dinosaur eggs. Some eggs need to be in the water. Some eggs stay on land.

Many animals that live in water lay eggs. Eggs in water are usually soft-shelled. Fish lay eggs in the water. Some fish eggs are heavy. They sink to the bottom of a lake or ocean. Other fish eggs are light and float. The male sea horse carries eggs in a pouch. The female octopus lays eggs in long strands. She hangs the strands from the roof of an underwater cave.

Other animals lay eggs on land. These eggs are usually hard-shelled. They contain food for the growing baby inside. Most birds lay eggs in nests. A nest helps the mother bird keep the eggs safe and warm. Some mother penguins lay eggs and give them to the father penguins to keep warm. The father penguin can stand on the ice with the egg on his feet for eight weeks!

Insects lay eggs too. Many insects lay eggs in sacs. They may attach the sacs to a leaf or branch.

Almost all mammals carry their babies inside their bodies until they are born alive. Only three species of mammals lay eggs: the duck-billed platypus and two types of spiny anteaters.

Eggs can be many sizes, colors, and textures. A fertilized egg contains the start of a new life.

Fill in the missing parts of the chart.

Animal	Description of Egg	Where Egg Is Laid or Placed
	soft-shelled	in pouch
	hard-shelled	in nest of twigs
	hard-shelled	on father's feet
octopus		
	in sacs	attached to leaves
fish	soft-shelled	

Draw an animal and its egg. Show where it would hatch and how it would stay protected.

Ruth's New Glasses

Ruth had a hard time seeing the board in class. Rosa sat next to her. Ruth asked Rosa to read the board each day. One day, their teacher said, "Ruth, I think that you should go to the eye doctor."

A few days later, Ruth went to the optometrist's office. On one side of the dark room was a chair with a machine in front of it. The doctor told Ruth to sit in the chair.

Dr. Riley pulled the machine over to Ruth. Part of the machine looked like a mask. Dr. Riley told Ruth to look through the mask and read some letters on the wall. As Dr. Riley turned some dials, the letters became blurry and then clear. Dr. Riley turned the dials until Ruth said that the letters were clear.

When Dr. Riley was finished, she took Ruth to another room. The optician helped Ruth and her mom pick out frames for her new glasses. Ruth picked out red frames. The optician told Ruth that her glasses would be ready in a few days. Ruth wished that she could wear her new glasses home.

In a few days, Ruth had her new glasses. She liked the way she looked with her glasses. She wore them to school.

"I'm glad that you finally have glasses," Rosa said. "I was getting tired of reading the board for you." They both laughed.

Answer each question from the story on page 52.

1. Why did Ruth's teacher think that Ruth should go to the

   eye doctor?_____

   _____

2. How did the eye doctor check Ruth's eyesight? _____

   _____

3. What do optometrists do?_____

   _____

4. What happened when Dr. Riley turned the dials on the machine?

   _____

5. What do opticians do? _____

   _____

6. Did Ruth like wearing her new glasses? _____

7. Why did Ruth and Rosa laugh at the end? _____

   _____

Emma's Dolls

Emma loved to sew. Her mom let her use fabric from her fabric box.

Emma cut two doll shapes from the fabric. She sewed them together. Then, she stuffed the doll. Emma painted eyes and a mouth with fabric paint. Next, she made hair with yarn. Emma sewed clothes for her doll. Emma named her doll Hazel.

Emma played with her new doll. She thought that her friends would like to have dolls like Hazel. Emma had an idea.

Emma asked her mom if she could have all of the fabric from the fabric box. Her mom said yes. Emma spent the next few days making dolls. Each doll had the same kind of body but different eyes, hair, and clothes. She named each doll. Finally, she had eight dolls and set up a store in her front yard.

Emma made a sign that read, *Dolls for sale! $5 each.* Emma put her dolls on a table. She put a card beside each doll with the doll's name on it. Then, she sat and waited.

Her friend Holly came to see what Emma was selling. Holly said that she would like to buy Hazel. She told Emma that she would go home to get her money.

When Holly returned, Emma was sitting at the table hugging the doll. Holly could tell something was wrong. "Are you OK?" Holly asked.

Answer each question from the story on page 54.

1. What was Emma's idea? _____

   _____

   _____

2. How does Emma feel about her dolls? _____

   _____

3. Have you ever made anything that you did not want to give

   away? Describe it. _____

   _____

   _____

4. Write an ending for the story. _____

   _____

   _____

   _____

   _____

   _____

Camping Trip

Thomas, his older brother Marcus, and their parents went on a camping trip. They found the perfect campsite beside a creek. Thomas and Marcus set up the tent while their parents unpacked the supplies for dinner. When the tent was set up, Thomas told his parents that he and Marcus wanted to go to the creek while the sun was still up. His father told them not to go too far from their campsite and to stay together.

Thomas and Marcus rolled up their pants and waded into the shallow water. Thomas used a stick to poke a few leaves on the creek bed. Then, he saw something that looked back at him. It was a snake! Thomas and Marcus jumped out of the water and raced back to camp. Thomas jumped into the tent and closed the flap.

Answer each question from the story on page 56.

1. What did Thomas and his family do first when they arrived at

   the campsite? _____

   _____

   _____

2. What did Thomas and Marcus do after that? _____

   _____

   _____

3. What did Thomas do last? _____

   _____

   _____

4. What do you think Thomas will do next? Write an ending for the story.

   _____

   _____

   _____

   _____

   _____

   _____

Embarrassing Moment

Nora was a <u>stubborn</u> little girl. She wanted to win a swim meet and a medal, but she was not willing to <u>train</u> for it. The <u>local</u> swimming pool offered free lessons, and she could have joined the swim team, but she decided that she was already good enough.

The first <u>competition</u> was <u>announced,</u> and Nora signed up. As she watched the races, she noticed that the swimmers started with a racing dive. She had never tried one of those.

Finally, it was her turn. She lined up on the starting block along with the other swimmers. The starting whistle was blown, and she held her nose and jumped into the water. It felt like an <u>eternity</u> before she surfaced. She wiped her eyes and saw that the rest of the swimmers had almost finished the race. She came in last place.

Her father wrapped her in a towel and held her close while she <u>sobbed</u>. She was really <u>embarrassed</u>.

Write each underlined word from page 58 next to its correct meaning.

1. _____ nearby

2. _____ forever

3. _____ cried

4. _____ practice

5. _____ contest between players or teams

6. _____ spoken publicly

7. _____ self-conscious and ashamed

8. _____ determined or unreasonable

What lesson did Nora learn? What might she do before her next meet?

_____

_____

_____

_____

_____

_____

> A nonsense word appears in each pair of sentences. Replace each nonsense word with a word that makes sense.

Nonsense Words

1. Isabel and Lucas rode their bikes to the **flibber** down the street.
   We watched Bridget **flibber** the car in the driveway.
   The nonsense word **flibber** is

   _____.

2. The little white dog is Tyrone's new **prackle**.
   Would you like to **prackle** this snake?
   The nonsense word **prackle** is

   _____.

3. My mom told me to **tirth** the baby to sleep.
   When we were on the beach, I found a beautiful **tirth** with a fossil imprint.
   The nonsense word **tirth** is _____.

4. Do not step on the **blape** on the sidewalk!
   When making breakfast, I can **blape** the eggs into the pan.
   The nonsense word **blape** is _____.

5. I cannot chew gum because it will **verg** to my braces.
   My dad asked me to pick up every **verg** in the yard.
   The nonsense word **verg** is _____.

6. I can tell time on my new **jeffa**.
   Will you **jeffa** me at my soccer game?
   The nonsense word **jeffa** is _____.